NATIONAL
GEOGRAPHIC

The Eve of Revolution

The Colonial Adventures of

Benjamin Wilcox

Barbara Burt

PICTURE CREDITS:
All images are from The Granger Collection, NY, except for cover (inset) and 6 (right inset) Art Resource, NY; pages 6–7, 8–9, 25, 28–29, 32–33, 34 North Wind Picture Archives; page 6 (left inset) The Newark Museum/Art Resource, NY; page 6 (center inset) National Museum of American Art Washington, DC/Art Resource, NY.

Cover: Charleston, South Carolina
Title page: Stamp Act riots in Boston
Contents page: Charleston, South Carolina

Library of Congress Cataloging-in-Publication Data
Burt, Barbara.
   The eve of Revolution: the colonial adventures of Benjamin Wilcox / by Barbara Burt.
      p. cm. (I am American)
   ISBN 0-7922-5211-X (pbk.)
   1. United States—Description and travel—Juvenile literature. 2. United States—History—Colonial period, ca. 1600–1775—Juvenile literature. 3. Boston (Mass.)—History—Colonial period, ca. 1600–1775—Juvenile literature. 4. Philadelphia (Pa.)—History—Colonial period, ca. 1600–1775—Juvenile literature. 5. Charleston (S.C.)—History—Colonial period, ca. 1600–1775—Juvenile literature. 6. United States—History—Revolution, 1775–1783—Causes—Juvenile literature. I. Title. II. Series

E163.B98 2003
973.3'1—dc21

                                  2002044941

Produced through the worldwide resources of the National Geographic Society, John M. Fahey, Jr., President and Chief Executive Officer; Gilbert M. Grosvenor, Chairman of the Board; Nina D. Hoffman, Executive Vice President and President, Books and Education Publishing; Ericka Markman, President, Children's Books and Education Publishing Group; Steve Mico, Vice President Education Publishing Group, Editorial Director; Marianne Hiland, Editorial Manager; Anita Schwartz, Project Editor; Tara Peterson, Editorial Assistant; Jim Hiscott, Design Manager; Linda McKnight, Art Director; Diana Bourdrez, Anne Whittle, Photo Research; Matt Wascavage, Manager of Publishing Services; Sean Philpotts, Production Coordinator.

Production: Clifton M. Brown III, Manufacturing and Quality Control

PROGRAM DEVELOPMENT
Gare Thompson Associates, Inc.

BOOK DESIGN
Herman Adler Design

Published by the National Geographic Society
1145 17th Street, N.W.
Washington, D.C. 20036-4688

Printed in Spain

Table of Contents

Seeds of Revolution

As the 13 British **colonies** of America grew, the colonists depended less and less on Britain. Some colonists resented being ruled by faraway Britain. They wanted to run things themselves and become **independent**.

In the 1760s, Britain decided to tax the colonists to pay for colonial defense. Britain passed the Stamp Act in 1765. This was a tax colonists had to pay each time they bought a newspaper or signed a legal document. A stamp showed that the tax had been paid.

Many colonists protested the Stamp Act. They said that colonial **legislatures,** or lawmaking bodies, had not agreed to this tax. People formed groups, such as the Sons of Liberty and the Daughters of Liberty, to fight against this act. Within a year, the Stamp Act was **repealed,** or canceled.

Then Britain passed another tax, the Townshend Acts. These acts forced the colonists to pay a tax on British **imports** of paint, tea, paper, glass, and lead. These were items that most colonists needed. In Boston

some groups decided to **boycott,** or refuse to buy, these British goods. Britain sent soldiers into Boston to enforce the laws and keep the peace. Tensions grew high.

The
13
Colonies

New Hampshire

Massachusetts

New York

Rhode Island
Connecticut

Pennsylvania

New Jersey
Delaware
Maryland

Virginia

North
Carolina

South
Carolina

Georgia

MEET THE WILCOX FAMILY

In 1769, the Wilcox family lives in the Massachusetts Bay Colony. Benjamin Wilcox is recovering from scarlet fever at his Uncle Robert's farm in Waterboro, Maine, part of the Massachusetts Bay Colony. When Benjamin is well, he decides to join his father at sea. Share his journey as he visits several colonies and discovers that many colonists want freedom from Britain.

Captain Henry Wilcox, father

Margaret Wilcox, 16

Benjamin Wilcox, 12

CHAPTER 1

Rumblings Reach the Countryside

Most people made a living in the colonies by farming. Colonists grew grains, vegetables, and fruits. They raised animals for wool, milk, and meat. They twisted rope from hemp plants and wove cloth from flax and wool. Farming was a hard but good life. Many colonial farmers were able to raise more crops than they needed for their own families. The surplus crops could be sold or traded for British or local goods.

Now the new taxes passed by the British made British goods very expensive. To buy the things they needed, farmers had to work even harder. They had to clear more fields and plant more crops. Not all farmers could afford to buy more land, seeds, and animals. Farmers thought the taxes were unfair. Many farmers began to resent the British.

Benjamin Wilcox was sent from his home in Boston to his uncle's farm in Waterboro, Maine, to recover from scarlet fever. He found farm life very different from life in the city. However, he saw the same resentment of Britain in the country that he had seen growing in Boston.

From Benjamin's journal
February 28, 1769

I finally feel strong again. I couldn't have lifted my quill pen to write a month ago. Today I spent the afternoon helping Uncle Robert. We cleared a new field. I still have to stop and rest often, but I am working.

Uncle says that with the new taxes, he must work even harder than before. It is hard for me to believe you can work any harder. But Uncle Robert says we must. Once the crops are sold, there will be little money left after paying the taxes on British goods. Aunt Mariah says we will buy fewer British goods. No tea for us.

Working on the farm is quite different from living in town. Here at Twin Oaks Farm, there are large fields to work. Work keeps us busy. We have little time or energy to protest against Britain. In Boston, people can gather on street corners or in inns. In the country, there are only farms with many miles between them. But we see soldiers here, too. Grandmother has written Aunt Mariah about the Daughters of Liberty. These are woman who refuse to buy British goods. Aunt Mariah thinks that is a good idea.

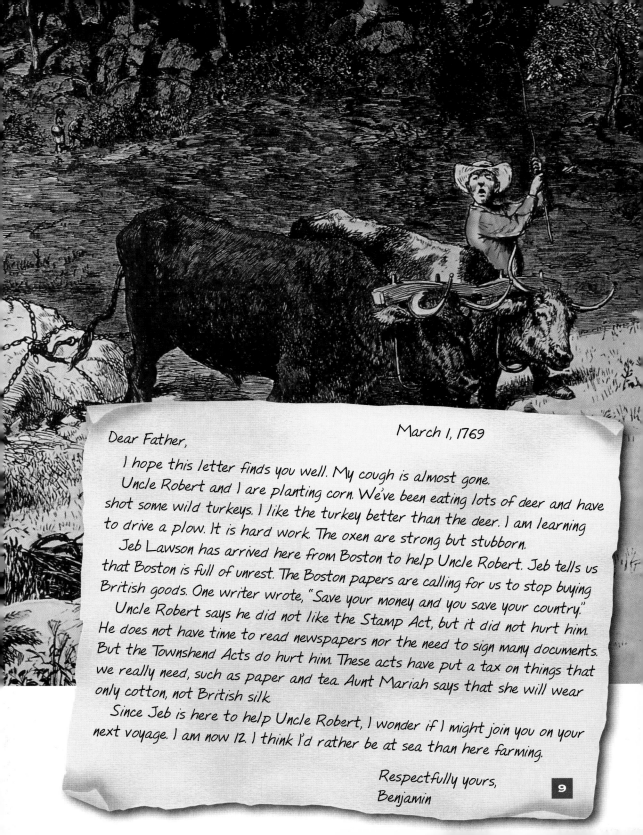

March 1, 1769

Dear Father,

I hope this letter finds you well. My cough is almost gone.

Uncle Robert and I are planting corn. We've been eating lots of deer and have shot some wild turkeys. I like the turkey better than the deer. I am learning to drive a plow. It is hard work. The oxen are strong but stubborn.

Jeb Lawson has arrived here from Boston to help Uncle Robert. Jeb tells us that Boston is full of unrest. The Boston papers are calling for us to stop buying British goods. One writer wrote, "Save your money and you save your country."

Uncle Robert says he did not like the Stamp Act, but it did not hurt him. He does not have time to read newspapers nor the need to sign many documents. But the Townshend Acts do hurt him. These acts have put a tax on things that we really need, such as paper and tea. Aunt Mariah says that she will wear only cotton, not British silk.

Since Jeb is here to help Uncle Robert, I wonder if I might join you on your next voyage. I am now 12. I think I'd rather be at sea than here farming.

Respectfully yours,
Benjamin

9

From Benjamin's journal
March 15, 1769

Jeb and Uncle Robert came home from town today quite upset. They said some British officers were watching them. Uncle Robert said he didn't know why. The soldiers' suspicious looks made him uneasy. He said that there now seems to be a difference between people living in Britain and those living here. Jeb calls us "Americans."

If things are tense here, they must be worse in Boston. Grandmother writes that she and Margaret have gone to meetings of the Daughters of Liberty. What will Grandmother do without her silks and teas?

For the first time, I am glad to be in the country and not in the city. Here we have no time for meetings or speeches. What I really want is to go to sea! Hopefully, I will soon. These troubles cannot follow me there.

Spinning and weaving cloth

Dear Son,   April 4, 1769

    Your letter reached me here in Boston. I am glad to hear you are finally well. Boston is a city in great confusion. Everyday someone speaks out against the British. Many come to the docks to protest against the British ships. I will be glad to be at sea.

    I am pleased that you want to join me. I share your feeling that being at sea is more exciting than farming. Uncle Robert would not agree. I would have you join me here in Boston for our first voyage to Philadelphia and then on to Charleston. However, I am not sure of our departure date. Because everyone is boycotting British goods, the colonists need our goods. We are very busy.

    Grandmother Wilcox was so pleased to hear you were coming home. She will be most pleased to see you. So will your sister Margaret.

    The ship is being loaded with cod, furniture, and lumber. The Sarah Margaret is as shipshape as can be. I am looking forward to using her new topsails.

                     With affection,
                     Your Father

Boston harbor

Colonists continued to speak out against the British. They protested the Townshend Acts almost daily. They continued to boycott British goods. British merchants were hurt by the colonists' refusal to buy their goods, but the Townshend Acts remained in place.

The British made other rules that angered the colonists. Some colonial farmers wanted to buy land west of the Appalachian Mountains. Land was cheaper there. The British would not permit it.

Suddenly British soldiers seemed to be everywhere. They were ordered to stop the many protests. This made the colonists resent the soldiers even more. Some colonists threw stones at them. They called the soldiers names, such as "lobsters" or "lobsterbacks" because of their red uniforms. As Benjamin arrives in Boston, the city is tense.

CHAPTER 2

Boston
Rebellion on the Rise

Boston was at the center of the **rebellion**. Newspaper articles and pamphlets spoke against British policies. British tax collectors were attacked. British goods were boycotted, burned, or dumped in the harbor. Small groups of rebels met in taverns and social clubs to plan their protests. Often, they gathered at street corners to protest the British.

From Benjamin's journal
April 26, 1769
I'm off to join Father in Boston! I leave in just four days. Hooray!

I think Uncle Robert understands. He says that living in Boston my first 12 years left me with more salt water than blood in my veins. Jeb will take my place.

I will take a ship south along the Maine coast to Boston. Captain Allen is the skipper. He's an old friend of Father's. I have missed the sea!

British occupation of Boston

From Benjamin's journal
April 30, 1769

At daybreak I met Captain Allen and his crew. We loaded the ship with the cargo bound for Boston. Then we set off. The voyage was quiet. When we sailed into Boston harbor, I was amazed at all the ships. Captain Allen said that the British ships might as well go home. No one will buy their goods.

On shore, I saw the grand Custom House. Near the wharves was a large and impressive red brick building, called Faneuil Hall. Meetings are held there. As I walked past, I could hear men protesting British rule. Soldiers were outside. It was odd seeing them with their guns. They looked ready for battle.

I found the *Sarah Margaret* and saw Father. He was busy and sent me off to Grandmother Wilcox's house on Beacon Hill. Boston is such a large and bustling town with winding streets. When I was younger, I feared getting lost. On the way, several men handed me pamphlets protesting British rule. I'll read them later.

I arrived to find Grandmother with her quilting group. I trust these Boston ladies will be spending more time sewing now that they are boycotting British goods.

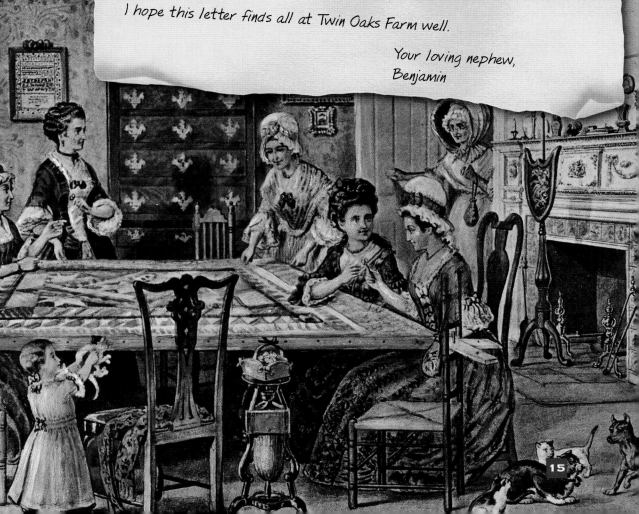

May 7, 1769

Dear Uncle Robert and Aunt Mariah,

As I write this letter, I am looking out the window of Grandmother Wilcox's house on Beacon Hill. Across Beacon Street is the Boston Common. Several cows are munching quietly on the spring grass. A group of men are gathered there, too. Unlike the cows, the men are angry. I can tell by their waving arms. Some of the men are finely dressed and wear powdered wigs. Uncle Robert, I can't picture you plowing in a wig! Each day, the protests seem to get worse.

As I look around at the comforts of Grandmother's house, I wonder what we are all protesting. I know taxes are bad. But we do not seem poor. The windows have silk curtains, and the shelves are full of gleaming silver. My bed is so plump with feathers that I instantly fall asleep at night. I am happy to see Margaret again, too. I do miss the whitewashed walls of your log home and the dried herbs hanging from the beams. Most of all, I miss our talks around the warm fire.

I hope this letter finds all at Twin Oaks Farm well.

Your loving nephew,
Benjamin

From Margaret's diary
May 10, 1769
Grandmother Wilcox is trying to convince Ben that he should become a minister instead of a sea captain. She says, "Life at sea is too hard and uncertain." This afternoon, she sent us to Cambridge to look at Harvard College. Cambridge is a small town across the Charles River from Boston. The college consists of a few brick buildings. The only students I saw were five boys about my age. They appeared rather pale and very serious. I do like reading and learning, but there are no colleges for women.

Harvard College

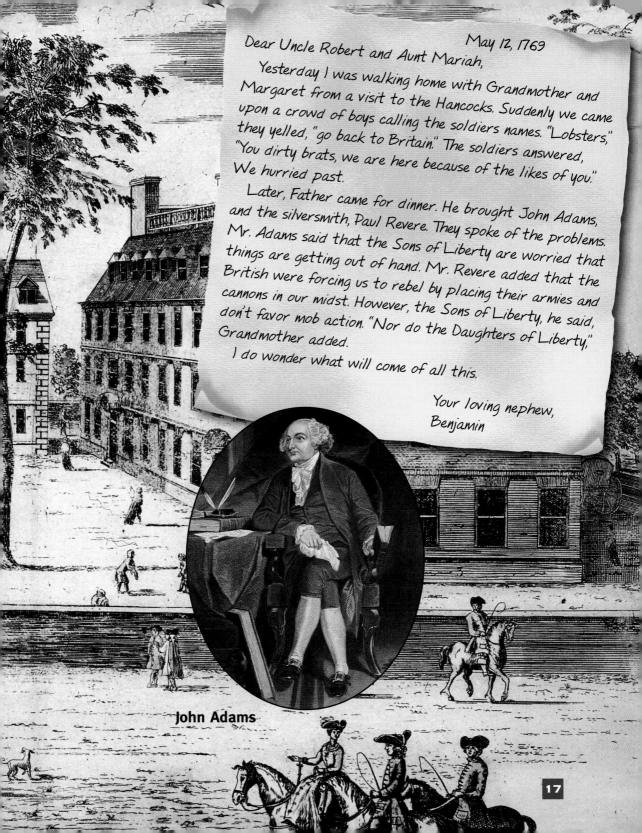

May 12, 1769

Dear Uncle Robert and Aunt Mariah,

Yesterday I was walking home with Grandmother and Margaret from a visit to the Hancocks. Suddenly we came upon a crowd of boys calling the soldiers names. "Lobsters," they yelled, "go back to Britain." The soldiers answered, "You dirty brats, we are here because of the likes of you." We hurried past.

Later, Father came for dinner. He brought John Adams, and the silversmith, Paul Revere. They spoke of the problems. Mr. Adams said that the Sons of Liberty are worried that things are getting out of hand. Mr. Revere added that the British were forcing us to rebel by placing their armies and cannons in our midst. However, the Sons of Liberty, he said, don't favor mob action. "Nor do the Daughters of Liberty," Grandmother added.

I do wonder what will come of all this.

Your loving nephew,
Benjamin

John Adams

The Sons and Daughters of Liberty continued their activities. Though most of the colonists were not yet demanding independence from Britian, their patience was wearing thin. The **occupation** of Boston by British troops increased the bad feeling. The more **radical**, or extreme, colonists only made things worse. Several fights betweeen colonists and soldiers took place. In one, an 11-year-old boy was shot. The British soldiers continued to carry out their drills in the city. The colonists continued to object.

Other cities reacted differently to British rule. Unlike Boston, Philadelphia wasn't full of rebels. Many merchants in Philadephia needed to sell their goods to the British. They did not join the boycott. Philadelphia's leaders, sush as Benjamin Franklin, believed that Britain should loosen its control over the colonies. They also believed that the colonies did not need to be independent. Franklin did poke fun at the British in *Poor Richard's Almanack*, his book of common sense sayings that he published each year.

CHAPTER 3

Philadelphia
City of Ideas and Inventions

William Penn founded the colony of Pennsylvania in 1681. He believed in **tolerance**, respecting the ideas and beliefs of all people. His very successful colony proved that freedom and fairness could lead to prosperity.

By 1769, Philadelphia, the capital of Pennsylvania, was the largest city in the American colonies. It had wealthy merchants and successful shop owners. Farmers carted their crops into the city from the rich land that surrounded it. Their corn, wheat, barley, rye, and fruits were bought by merchants and shipped to ports both north and south.

Prosperity drew thinkers and inventors to Philadelphia. Among them was the amazing Benjamin Franklin, who arrived as a teenager. Franklin invented many things, such as the Franklin stove and the lightning rod. He was the postmaster of Philadelphia and helped to found the first fire department.

Philadelphia harbor

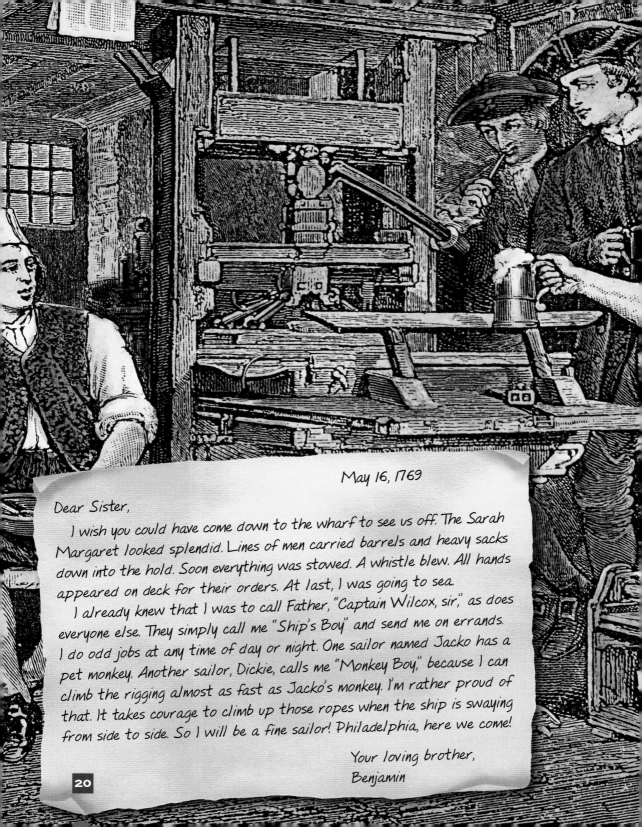

May 16, 1769

Dear Sister,

I wish you could have come down to the wharf to see us off. The Sarah Margaret looked splendid. Lines of men carried barrels and heavy sacks down into the hold. Soon everything was stowed. A whistle blew. All hands appeared on deck for their orders. At last, I was going to sea.

I already knew that I was to call Father, "Captain Wilcox, sir," as does everyone else. They simply call me "Ship's Boy" and send me on errands. I do odd jobs at any time of day or night. One sailor named Jacko has a pet monkey. Another sailor, Dickie, calls me "Monkey Boy," because I can climb the rigging almost as fast as Jacko's monkey. I'm rather proud of that. It takes courage to climb up those ropes when the ship is swaying from side to side. So I will be a fine sailor! Philadelphia, here we come!

Your loving brother,
Benjamin

From Benjamin's journal
May 22, 1769

We docked in Philadelphia. This morning, I helped Father deliver paper to the print shop where *Poor Richard's Almanack* is printed. We met Mr. Benjamin Franklin there. He is the famous author of this popular book. Now he spends much of his time with his inventions. He is also a member of the Pennsylvania Assembly. He was disappointed that the Pennsylvania Assembly didn't vote for the boycott as Massachusetts did.

Mr. Franklin was wearing a strange pair of glasses with two lenses in each eyepiece. He let me look through them. The view through the top half of each was blurry. From the bottom half, it was even blurrier! He says he can see both the food on his plate and his friends across the table when wearing these glasses. He calls them bifocals! Mr. Franklin keeps inventing things!

Mr. Franklin asked if I liked reading and writing. I said that I did, which seemed to please him. He told me that reading and writing had taken him from being a poor apprentice to a man of independent means. Then he offered me an apprenticeship in his print shop. He wanted me to learn the printing trade. I will think on it. Newspapers are important. And Mr. Franklin is a great man.

May 23, 1769

Dear Sister,

You would have been amazed to see the sight Father and I saw this morning. Returning from Mr. Franklin's offices, we noticed smoke coming from a warehouse. Suddenly, a group of men dashed by. Next came two horse-drawn carriages carrying water tanks and hoses. When the men got to the fire, some formed a bucket brigade. Others pumped water and aimed the hoses. The fire was out before it had done much damage.

One of the men told us Mr. Franklin had organized a volunteer fire company. "When the firehouse bell rings," said the man, "we drop everything and run to the firehouse." The man also told us that Mr. Franklin had started a police force. No wonder one feels safe in Philadelphia.

Your brother, Benjamin

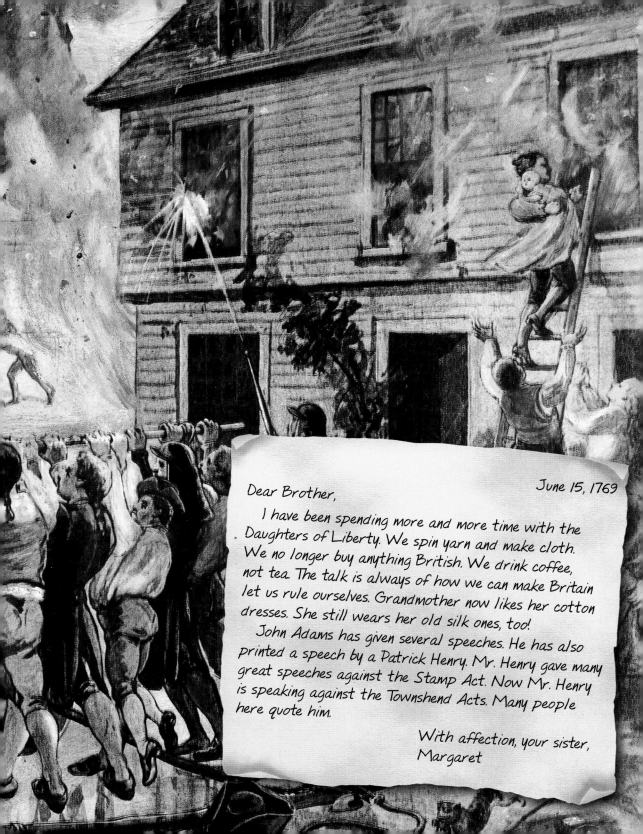

June 15, 1769

Dear Brother,

I have been spending more and more time with the Daughters of Liberty. We spin yarn and make cloth. We no longer buy anything British. We drink coffee, not tea. The talk is always of how we can make Britain let us rule ourselves. Grandmother now likes her cotton dresses. She still wears her old silk ones, too!

John Adams has given several speeches. He has also printed a speech by a Patrick Henry. Mr. Henry gave many great speeches against the Stamp Act. Now Mr. Henry is speaking against the Townshend Acts. Many people here quote him.

With affection, your sister,
Margaret

State House (Independence Hall)

Colonial Philadelphia was a beautiful city with many fine brick buildings. Brick was used to avoid the threat of fire. The most impressive building was called the State House then. Today it is called Independence Hall. The Declaration of Independence was first read there.

As time passed, Philadelphia became more involved in the rebellion. Its leaders began to speak out against Britain. In 1774, representatives to the First Continental Congress met in Philadelphia. Every colony sent representatives except Georgia. The representatives came to protest unfair British laws. Philadelphia was to become the center for many more such meetings.

Its most famous citizen was Benjamin Franklin. He was a great politician and statesman. As the rebellion grew, he was a leader people listened to.

Benjamin enjoyed his time in Philadelphia with Mr. Franklin. He looked forward to their next stop, Charleston. Charleston was quite different from both Boston and Philadelphia. In Charleston, Ben was to see a very different way of life.

CHAPTER 4

Charleston
A Different Way of Life

In the steamy climate of South Carolina, rice, **indigo**, and tobacco are crops that grow well. Some farmers had huge **plantations** of hundreds of acres on which these crops were grown. They had difficulty finding enough workers to tend their fields. They began to buy enslaved Africans to do this work. On some of the big plantations, there were ten enslaved Africans for every free person.

Plantation owners became very wealthy. Many of them lived most of the year in splendid Charleston. They left the countryside to escape the heat and the disease-carrying mosquitoes.

From Benjamin's journal
June 16, 1769

The weather kept us at anchor in Philadelphia harbor for an extra day. The next morning the wind finally sprang up and we were able to set out. After about five hours of sailing, the wind became much stronger. Father ordered all hands on deck to secure the hatches and cargo and lower the sails.

Then a sad tragedy took place. Jacko's monkey had climbed the rigging beside his master. A pole swung around and caught the monkey in the side. It flung the poor creature through the air and into the angry sea. I'm glad no one could be blamed for the monkey's death.

Under only a few storm sails, we are now plowing through the water. We're making the fastest speed I've seen since coming aboard. We are riding down the waves like a sled down a snow-covered hill. That explains my funny-looking handwriting.

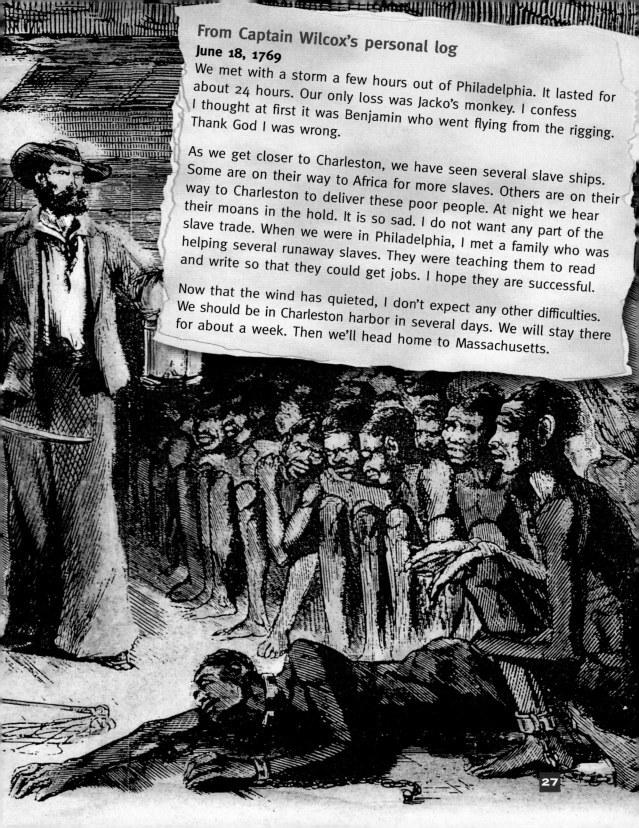

From Captain Wilcox's personal log
June 18, 1769

We met with a storm a few hours out of Philadelphia. It lasted for about 24 hours. Our only loss was Jacko's monkey. I confess I thought at first it was Benjamin who went flying from the rigging. Thank God I was wrong.

As we get closer to Charleston, we have seen several slave ships. Some are on their way to Africa for more slaves. Others are on their way to Charleston to deliver these poor people. At night we hear their moans in the hold. It is so sad. I do not want any part of the slave trade. When we were in Philadelphia, I met a family who was helping several runaway slaves. They were teaching them to read and write so that they could get jobs. I hope they are successful.

Now that the wind has quieted, I don't expect any other difficulties. We should be in Charleston harbor in several days. We will stay there for about a week. Then we'll head home to Massachusetts.

June 25, 1769

Dear Margaret,

   We have finally arrived in Charleston. What an amazing place! Flowers are everywhere, and the houses are as colorful as the blossoms! Pink, blue, yellow, green. I have never seen such beautiful buildings. Many have these fancy iron balconies and railings.

   The people, too, are grand. Their carriages are fancy and their clothes are very fine. Many of the richest men own huge plantations. Because it is so unbearably hot away from the sea, many plantation owners spend most of the year in beautiful Charleston. I don't blame them. We have had a taste of the very hot weather. An entire summer of it would be unbearable.

   Many Africans live in Charleston. As I walk down the streets of the town, I see many more black faces than white. Some of the Africans are dressed in fine clothing, but others are in barely more than rags. I cannot tell for sure, but I believe that few of the Africans in South Carolina are free.

   I hope this letter finds you well and in good spirits.

                                        Your brother,
                                        Ben

From Captain Wilcox's personal log
June 27, 1769

Ben and I rode outside the city today. I wanted to see what the countryside was like. It is so different than Massachusetts. There are few roads.

We went to dinner with Mr. Jackson. His house is huge. The rooms are filled with furniture from Britain and France. He says that his house is small compared to some of his neighbors. To me, it seemed like a small city. It had all kinds of shops, and a blacksmith, stables, and gardens. Mr. Jackson has over 300 acres. He also has many slaves to work his land. The slaves in the house looked well fed and cared for. But I must confess that I did not like being served by slaves.

They served us many rice dishes. Rice is one of the main crops here. I liked the rice and beans the best. As we rode home, I noticed some small shacks in the back of the big house. Ben and I realized that this was where the slaves lived. We rode back to the city in silence.

June 30, 1769

Dear Daughter,

I have learned much about indigo and rice since stopping here in Charleston. One interesting fact is that growing indigo was first encouraged by a lady, Mistress Eliza Pinckney. She was born in the West Indies and educated in England. Later, she was left in charge of a South Carolina plantation. She began to experiment with indigo. Today, indigo is one of South Carolina's most important crops. The colony exports over one million pounds of indigo a year. So you see, women are very important in business. I just wish the crops did not depend on the work of slaves.

In several days, we will sail to Boston to sell our cargo of rice and indigo. I've also picked up something special for you here in Charleston. Don't worry—it was not made by the British. I wouldn't dare to suggest you break the boycott.

With affection,
Your Father

Charleston harbor

From Benjamin's journal
July 2, 1769

Father and I ate in Charleston. We had a fine meal of fish, meat, and vegetables. We had apple pie for dessert.

Later, we walked around the city. Charleston is very lively at night. The houses are all lit up. The people here like to get together and have fun. Father says it is because the plantations are so far apart.

We watched the stars fill the sky. I think that Charleston is a beautiful city, but I miss Boston. I do not like the heat here or the fancy ways of the rich.

Father and I met a man who owns a silver shop. He used to be a sailor. He and Father traded sea stories. Then he sold Father a wonderful silver box. It was made by a local man who had studied under Paul Revere. Father will give the box to Margaret.

I count the stars as I fall asleep in my hammock.

Spanish slave ship

From Benjamin's journal
July 4, 1769
Last night, I was standing watch on the *Sarah Margaret* when an African man boarded our ladder. He spoke the King's English. He asked us to hide him and bring him north with us. His name is Thomas Smithton. He says he was a free man in Barbados. But when the slave ship *Aurora* stopped in Barbados last month, he was kidnapped and brought to South Carolina. He finally managed to escape. His wrists and ankles are raw from the chains he had to wear. He seems an honorable man. Father has agreed to bring him to Massachusetts. He is now hiding in my berth.

From Captain Wilcox's personal log
July 6, 1769
I have had several interesting conversations with Thomas Smithton. He is clearly a learned man. He traveled to England ten years ago. In Barbados he was a well-regarded furniture craftsman.

It is so hard for me to understand the things I see here in Charleston. This morning, I traveled nine miles up the Ashley River to Drayton Hall. We were arranging a delivery of rice for shipment to Boston. The grounds are beautiful, with trees and gardens and walkways. The house is the most elegant I've ever seen. It is grander than the home of Mr. Jackson. But still, it doesn't seem fair to me that slaves do all the work.

Drayton Hall, South Carolina

South Carolina wasn't the only colony with slaves. Even as far north as Massachusetts, some colonists kept slaves. Most people frowned on the practice. Still when the patriots spoke about liberty and justice, few of them thought about the enslaved Africans.

The Southern colonies continued to grow crops, such as tobacco, cotton, and rice that used slave labor. As time passed, the southern way of life became very different from life in the North. The plantations became more and more dependent on slaves. Slavery itself became a business.

Ben and his father returned to Boston. Over the next year, tensions between the colonists and the British continued to grow. Boston was a city waiting to explode.

CHAPTER 5

Tensions Erupt
The Boston Massacre

On the evening of March 5, 1770, tensions between the British soldiers and the Bostonians finally erupted. A crowd gathered outside and began insulting a British guard. British soldiers went to his rescue. The frightened soldiers fired their guns into the crowd. Crispus Attucks, probably a runaway slave, and two other colonists were killed. Two others were wounded and later died. This event became known as the Boston **Massacre.**

The Boston Massacre became famous throughout the colonies. John Adams and Josiah Quincy, Jr., two Sons of Liberty, defended the soldiers in court. They convinced the jury that the soldiers had feared for their lives. They had fired in self-defense. Adams and Quincy wanted the world to know that the colonists were fair-minded and obeyed the law.

Across the Atlantic, the British repealed most of the Townshend Acts. It was too late. The damage to the relationship between Britain and the colonies had already been done.

From Margaret's diary
March 5, 1770
Today is a day we will never forget. We were talking in Grandmother's library when we heard the church bells ring. That seemed odd. We went to the window. People were running to the Customs House. Father, Ben, and I followed the crowd. As we neared the Customs House, we could see a group of British soldiers. Colonists were pelting them with snowballs and calling them names. The whole crowd was screaming, "Lobsterbacks, lobsterbacks!" Suddenly, the soldiers fired into the crowd. We saw men fall! Later, we learned that three men had been killed and others wounded. What will happen now?

May 10, 1770

Dear Uncle Robert,

I hope that this letter finds all of you at Twin Oaks well. I am sure that you are working hard clearing more fields and getting ready to plant.

Boston seems calmer now. Father says that the repeal of the Townshend Acts shows that Britain is finally listening to us. Grandmother does not agree. She is still angry over the Boston Massacre. That is what that terrible fight is now called. Her friend John Adams will defend the British soldiers. I wonder if they will get a fair trial. Luckily, the governor has ordered most of the soldiers out of Boston. Still, Father will not let any of us walk around town alone.

We hope that you and Aunt Mariah can come to visit soon.

Your loving nephew,
Benjamin

Boston, Massacre
Crispus Attucks at left center

From Margaret's diary

June 10, 1770

John Adams was here for dinner last night. He said that many are angry with him for defending the British soldiers. Mr. Adams feels we must show Britain that we can be fair. Grandmother did not agree. She thinks that the British should go home. Mr. Adams said he is glad she is not speaking at the town meetings. She would start a war. Father kept quiet. He did say that war should be avoided, if possible. Ben thinks that everything Mr. Adams says is wonderful. I am not sure what I think. I want us to be free, but I would hate to see Ben go to war. Must people die for us to be free?

From Benjamin's journal

June 11, 1770

The streets are finally quiet. Father lets us go for walks alone once more. I go to the docks. Somehow, the sea is not as exciting to me as it was. I like listening to men like John Adams talk. I think that the soldiers should get a fair trial. I admire Mr. Adams for what he is doing. He has suggested that maybe I would like to study law. I like that idea.

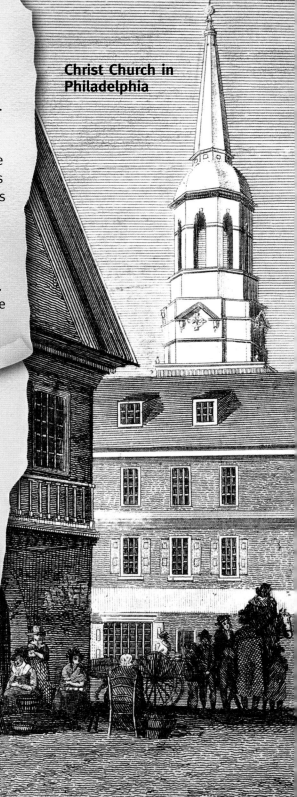

Christ Church in Philadelphia

Epilogue

The hated tax on tea remained. In 1773, angry colonists, wearing disguises, boarded a British ship and dumped over 300 chests of tea into the harbor. This event was known as the Boston Tea Party. The furious British then closed Boston harbor. They passed laws to make the colonists pay for the British soldiers' housing and food. Colonial town meetings were **banned,** or forbidden. The colonists called these laws the Intolerable Acts.

Most colonists were finally convinced of the need to fight for freedom. On July 4, 1776, representatives to the Second Continental Congress **adopted** the Declaration of Independence. It announced the separation of the 13 colonies from Britain to become the United States. The Revolutionary War had begun.

Benjamin joined the American army. He served under General George Washington. After the war, Benjamin became a lawyer. When Thomas Jefferson became President in 1800, Benjamin went to work for him. He moved to the new capital, Washington, D.C. There he lived until his death.

Margaret married one of John Hancock's cousins. She wrote about her life in the colonies and about the Boston Massacre. She also spoke out for the establishment of colleges for women. She wanted her daughters to be well educated. The Wilcox family were proud Americans.

Glossary

adopt - to accept an idea or a way of doing things

ban - to forbid something

boycott - to refuse to buy something or to take part in something as a way of making a protest

colony - a place that is ruled by a distant country

imports - goods brought in from another country for sale or use

independent - free from the control or rule of others

indigo - a plant from which a blue dye is made

legislature - a body of people that has the power to make or pass laws

massacre - the brutal, bloody killing of many people

occupation - the taking over and controlling of a country or an area by an army

plantation - a large farm found in warm climates where crops such as coffee, tea, rubber, and cotton are grown

radical - favoring extreme change

rebellion - armed fight against a government

repeal - to do away with officially

tolerance - willingness to respect the customs, ideas, or beliefs of others